# Rivers Are Coming

Essays and Poems on Healing

Minaa B.

Rivers Are Coming

By Minaa B.

Library of Congress Control Number: 2016907358

CreateSpace Independent Publishing Platform, North Charleston, SC

—

ISBN-10: 1532727534
ISBN-13: 978-1532727535

This book is for the ones who never left.

I admire your hearts for being courageous enough to get wet with me within my storms.

I cry rivers for you. And I hope these sweet tears plant seeds of love, hope, and prosperity within your gardens; may you be blessed tremendously.

Mother: You have been good to me. I hope this book sings a song that you can dance to. I love you.

Pa: Thank you for all that you gave me and continue to give me; may you rest peacefully.

# Contents

Behold, I will do a new thing,

Now it shall spring forth; shall you not know it?

I will even make a road in the wilderness and rivers in the desert.

—Isaiah 43:19 NKJV

.

# Part I

# Introduction

I am looking for warm words to fill these pages. I have searched deeply within for my voice that has the power to flood this universe and turn it upside down. As I speak, the moon moans back to me, and the sun sings its song of praise within my ear.

The blue that is hidden within the distance comes rushing toward me with a surge of passion and wonder, sending vibrations of warmth down my spine and filling my body with ecstasy. With every breath I taste the sweetness of truth, and I am in awe at how satisfying self-expression can be for the soul. I have allowed myself to collide with the outside world, no longer hidden underneath the surface of my struggles or wrapped in a web full of self-doubt and depression. I am made alive again. Dipped in God and created new.

This body that was once burdened by the weight

of suffering, generational strongholds, mistakes, and an unsound mind has found peace again. Death no longer dwells here. Every day I am learning to dance to the beat of my own rhythm, and as I sing my praises aloud, the quiet within me subsides, and I become more and more familiar with the woman who lives within my reflection.

The time has come for me to make my reentry into the world. I have magic to produce, fields to frolic through, flowers to pick, art to make, power to influence with, and rivers to dance in. This book is about change and radical transformation. Your river is coming. Change is coming. May these words find you and rest deeply within your soul.

# The River

As a young child, I once feared the waves of the sea and the hymns of the ocean because I felt too small to go up against something so vast and beautiful, resilient and robust. I once saw myself as pollution and considered it a sin to invite my toxicity into something so marvelously created. Learning how to swim brought forth challenges that only a nurtured and healed self-esteem could fix and use to help keep me afloat.

Struggling with depression took away my ease and confidence. I was robbed of my ability to see my beauty and my aptitude to bend and break without losing my worth. At the tender age of six, I remember uttering the words "I hate myself" as I looked at the young queen who stood in front of the mirror. Naively, this internal hate started with how I was perceived in the eyes of six-year-olds.

According to my peers and the playground bullies, I lacked cuteness and tenderness because of my tall and slinky frame. My wide teeth and overbite earned me the nickname Bugs Bunny, and I became the punching bag for cheap jokes and superficial laughter. I was the ugly duckling that waddled around the schoolyard, and at an age where you don't know any better, I believed the hateful things that these young kiddies spoke over me.

As time traveled, it seemed as though my heart never healed from the sting of torment that it was subjected to, and through my phases of development, I found myself broken to pieces and shattered by so much hurt and pain. I had no love for myself, and it showed through the connections that I fostered with people who had no respect or good intentions for me. I gave so much of myself away to others and received nothing in return except my heart in my hands and my soul thirsting for grace.

At the age of sixteen, my body no longer wanted to call this earth home. One cut turned into two, two turned into three, three into four, and the tally marks on my wrist became evidence of my depression and my hopeless state of mind. Pain was my love language; I was well versed in it. My tongue knew only the taste of bitterness because I had spoken so ill of myself for practically half of my life.

Depression and cutting were my secrets, and they spiraled into an addiction. My addict behaviors were catching up to me, and I could no longer stay hidden or silence my troubles. I never saw myself in counseling, but that is where I found myself. I didn't know how to talk about how badly my heart was hurting because I never learned how to speak my own truths. What I call depression is a feeling of emptiness, unworthiness, fear of abandonment, lack of self-recognition, ineffectiveness, lack of confidence, and the tragic loss of childhood. It hurts to admit that my world was once shaped by the beliefs of others—but that is my reality, that is my truth.

I began to walk toward wholeness on my journey when I realized my pain was what was going to give me access to freedom. For so long, I ignored what my heart was telling me out of shame and the fear of not being loved by the masses. In the midst of my storms, I was too blind to see that loving myself was the ultimate prize, and that thought benefited me more than anything else this world could offer. The process of learning how to love oneself is exactly that, a learned behavior. It is a process, and it requires openness and truth and a spirit vulnerable enough to receive correction, while we also tap into the knowledge and the power that is stored within our bodies that enables us to be one with ourselves, and guides us on our journey.

When I was nineteen, my father died, and at his funeral we played "Change Is Gonna Come," by Otis Redding, as a tribute. For years after his death, every time I heard that song play, my bones shook, and my heart sank to the floor. The thought of my father no longer being a present figure in my life rocked me and ripped me to shreds every time I had to accept the truth that he was gone. This Otis Redding song was one of his favorite tunes, and though it hurt to hear the song, as time heals all wounds, I eventually began to adore every lyric, every melody, every tone, and every harmony of this form of art communicated through sound. My father had given me a gift during his passing that I have now stumbled upon years later. He taught me how to swim in a sea of uncertainty and taught me how to trust the waves of the sea as we swim deeper into the unknown.

Change is often hidden beneath struggle. And I believe strength is always birthed within weakness. It is birthed within pain, heartache, tragedy, and loss. I have come to understand that what once broke you has the potential to serve you. Don't disregard downfalls or struggles; everything that flows through the body has purpose. And I found my purpose when I allowed my feet to travel toward the unknown and placed my hope within the waves of the one who is steadfast and unwavering.

As I come face to face with the river and look toward the distance of the sea, I see myself in the vastness of this world. I see my reflection in the sun as I recognize the light that dwells within me. My beauty is unfolded wave by wave as I recognize my being as fearfully and wonderfully made. The roughness of the sea and the rhythms of the waters no longer frighten me, for as I stumbled upon my worthiness, I also stumbled upon my ability to be resilient and robust enough to face any storm that tries to wear me down. I too am marvelously created, and I deserve to have a spot on this earth.

The river dominates its territory because it is fully aware of its place within creation. We are all full just like the river, full of thoughts, words, wonders, art, creativity, and love, and we all carry an abundant flow of these things to help guide us through our journey.

As we attempt this thing known as growth and evolution, it is important to note the significance of seasons and how they fluctuate in our lives. Change occurs on an everyday basis, and the point to this thing called humanness is to transform daily, but never to forget where you are held just like the seas, just like the oceans, just like the river.

The river is symbolic of rhythm and grace, movement and transformation. It's the becoming of something, the extension of something, and the letting go of something. May we all come face to face with the river.

## Waltz

I just wanted to dance in the chaos.

I just wanted to run wild in the darkness of the
night underneath the universe.

I just wanted to taste the sweetness of my tears

produced from my misery.

I just truly wanted to feel for the

first time what it meant

to be human

to be broken

to struggle,

to live in a world where people would

allow me the entitlement of having feelings.

I was robbed for way too long.

It's time for me to take back

what is rightfully mine.

## The Loving

Understand that life

is made up of seasons,

which means going through

the storm is inevitable.

But there is beauty in knowing that

despite your rainiest days

and darkest nights,

the stars never cease to shine for you,

the sun never fails to rise for you,

the moon never fails to radiate for you,

and that is because you are loved.

## Wholeness

Becoming one with my

darkness has been

beautiful for my soul.

# Thief in the Night

Please don't rob me

of my ability to feel

because you can't

handle my truths.

## Lessons

I am thankful

for the lessons

that were found within

the fragmented pieces

of my brokenness.

Without them, I

wouldn't have been

made whole.

## Full Moon

Trust your rhythms.

Be in touch with your

moods and your moon.

You will go through waning phases,

which are symbolic of releasing,

preparing your heart to receive.

Be at peace with your endings,

and prepare your heart for

nature's offerings.

## Liberated

Change will often disturb energies, sending vibrations through the body that result in the alterations of moods and patterns. Support the process by touching yourself with grace.

Your mind is slowly detaching from what no longer serves you, and this is an act of liberation for your soul. As you evolve inwardly, admire your heart for its ability to bend and break yet still travel through phases and seasons within the journey.

## Love Language

Honesty is the best form

of communication

that you will ever have

with yourself—

practice it daily.

Authenticity is what

makes you feel more alive.

So sing your praises, and make your

petitions known to the universe.

Honor your gospel,

and be unashamed to

share your tidings.

## Wanderer

The discovery of self

comes from the

tragedy of

loss.

## Tired of Being Broken

Go where your

heart is wanted.

That will save you

the ache of

breaking

again.

# Tame Your Tongue

Stop giving the devil

a song to dance to.

## Note to Self

Be kind to yourself; you are trying. Stop discrediting yourself; you are trying. You may be facing opposition, and I know you are going through the storm, but I also see the courage in your eyes and the fire in your heart. You're going to do great things with that life of yours. So keep going; the battle has already been won.

## The Killing

It is much easier for the human mind

to view uncertainty as dangerous

rather than a glorious awakening

into unknown territory.

Instead of choosing to anoint our feet

and walk toward the unknown,

we would rather stay bound

by chains and stand still

in our fears and worries.


But that, my love,

that is not living;

that's more like a

spiritual suicide.

## The Fall

I hope you know that

even in your brokenness

you are still worthy of love.

Love is magical enough to

wrap you in its arms

even when times are rough and

you are covered in wounds.

I want you to know that love is

limitless, and its options are bottomless.

Don't be afraid, my love.

Love is still willing to catch you.

You just have to be willing to fall.

# Feelings Are Not Facts

Managing our feelings and emotions can be tricky. Our feelings have power—they help us keep our rhythms and be in tune with our humanness. But what you need to know about your feelings is that when you give them too much power, they can disrupt, alter, and deceive you from knowing who you are and who you are destined to become. How many times have we felt small? Unsure? Not good enough? Or not brave enough? And then we turn around and declare ourselves as small, insignificant, not good enough, and incapable. How you see yourself can be a fundamental element to how you "feel" about yourself. And if you feel small, then you shall be what you feel.

Your feelings should not serve you or stop you

from cultivating a life of purpose. Ultimately, your feelings should not be the deity of your life, because sometimes our feelings do not align with our purpose—and embracing your purpose, not your feelings, should be your weapon of warfare. Purpose is real, purpose disrupts reality, purpose changes lives, purpose is why you were created. And sometimes, purpose is something that you cannot feel.

Know that you have a right to your feelings—just don't allow your feelings to be seated on the throne.

## Seasons

Depression is a story

that has an ending.

## Oceans

Don't be afraid

to walk toward

the bigger picture.

Toward the unknown,

toward mystery.

Your feet will not fail you, and

your steps will never misguide you.

Allow yourself to experience the

whole world, not just pieces of it.

Let your ship sail, and trust where the

journey takes you.

## Brave Heart

If you got out of bed

this morning,

give yourself

a round of applause.

Being human

can be

hard sometimes.

## Holy Water

I got baptized last night.

I sat in a pool of my tears and drank the
blood of my ancestors while I broke bread
and gave thanks to God for leading me to the
river.

My flesh encounters rock after rock as my feet
wander deeper into the rushing waters; wave
after wave knocks them back.

I hear the river screaming at me to get on my
knees, arch my back, and bend my waist while
I drown and reemerge made new.

Made whole.

I lie on my back and watch my demons drift
afar, carried away by the river.

Glory be to God.

# To Build a Home

Sometimes home isn't a place built out of stone or of wooden floors, or a place with windows and chairs. Sometimes home isn't a city or a neighborhood. Sometimes home is found simply in the souls we come across, in the dusk, and in the recollection of memories that we share with other beings. Sometimes home is found on the journey, on the ship sailing toward self-discovery. It is where you find serenity, where you find peace, where the doors groan day and night, a dwelling place for your heart.

And most of the time home is simply a place that we build.

## Take Me Deeper

I like the idea of being able

    to live among the unknown.

I like to keep the door open to the dark.

The only desire within my heart is to get lost

    in a glorious surrender,

to release myself from the burden of concealment.

I've been broken down to pieces many times in my

life, and as I mold myself back together, I always

seem to find a piece of treasure

even within my brokenness.

I like that the dark and I have

    something in common;

we both know how to conceal the beautiful

    wonders of this world, of our intimate parts.

If only humans would be brave enough to

step into the darkness,

this world would be full of riches,

for they too would find the

most wonderful hidden treasures

within their soul, within this universe.

## Suffocated

Stop letting your mistakes

hold you hostage.


Stop letting your past

hold you hostage.

## Black Magic

The pictures on the pamphlets

and the images within my TV screen

told me that brown girls don't struggle

with depression.

This disease is painted on white bodies;

my ancestors taught me better than to let my

mind be the death of me.

But I'm dying.

And as you nail my mouth shut, I feel my unborn
children suffering within my womb.

They want to know, why I am hurting them? And
they are not even born yet. Why do I make them
suffer? My, what have we done?

## Paradox

The art of letting go

is an act of both

rewarding your spirit

and opening your soul

to pain and heartache.

# Beautiful Bride

All my life I hid myself from the world because I wasn't sure of who could handle all my mess and me. I walked around clothed in shame and full of fear. But the more I tried to hide, the sicker I became, and I feared that people would see my self-inflicted battle scars. I struggled with sharing my story and in the midst of my darkness, I was slowly dying from the inside out. I knew that if I wanted to wake up to see another morning, to tell my parents I love them, to be there for my friends, to potentially be a wife and a mother, and to live the life that I knew I was capable of living, I knew I couldn't live a life of paranoia and secrecy anymore. I needed help.

My journey to recovery is still happening this very moment. I still struggle with fear. I still struggle with anxiety. I still struggle with isolation. And I still struggle with depression. But if there is one thing that I can say has helped my journey, it would be the moment I unveiled myself like a bride to her groom. It was the moment I undressed myself and allowed the world to see my nakedness, my scars, my flaws, and my imperfections. It was the moment that I decided that I wanted to give my life its best chance.

When I realized that there is no such thing as failing at life, I realized I had nothing to lose, for opportunity comes every single day. Our mess-ups are not permanent. The sun never stops rising, and our struggles don't define us; they equip us for the journey.

## Stay Soft

My spine

has been broken

by my burdens

and bones

made weak.

I have never

once felt so

fragile

yet so awakened

all in the same moment.

## Lessons from Flowers

Your magic is always unfolding.

It does not wither away

just because others choose

not to love you.

# Because I Tended to My Garden

They can see something

different in me

compared to the girl I once was.

I radiate differently.

My energy is warm

and my smiles are authentic.

People want to know how I changed

and I simply tell them I evolved.

My roots were struggling for a long time,

but I stopped picking away at my petals

and I allowed myself

to bloom.

# Decisions

You cannot be

a worrier

and

a warrior

at the same time.

## Strong Black Woman

Someone once told me

that the color of my skin can

heal me from any curse.

They say my brownness

is the reason why I am strong.

So why am I still hurting?

## Awakened

The day I woke up with a burning desire in my heart to give my life its best chance is the moment that I walked away from fear and into the arms of hope. I am the face of many suicide attempts, depression and anxiety, and I am the stigma that society fears. But above all else, I choose not to be the face of the person who gave up.

# The Elephant in the Room

A man once shared a story with me about a documentary he watched on circus elephants. When the elephant is in its prime stage of development, the trainer wraps a rope around one of its legs, and on the other end of that rope is a stick welding it into the ground so that the elephant is bound and cannot escape. The baby elephant reacts to its circumstances in its most normal way possible, by weeping and crying, tugging and fighting, but it cannot break free.

This process is done every day, and as the elephant gets older, he gives up on fighting and becomes adjusted to the idea that he will never be free. Little does he know he could snap that rope with one tug and wander freely but he doesn't, because from infancy the elephant trained his mind to believe that his circumstances would always remain the same, and in the midst of his struggles, he lost his ability to have hope.

I worry that humans also believe their restraints are permanent. I worry that most people believe failure is final, and they give up on trying, they give up on bettering themselves, and they give up on their journeys. Our fears suffocate us, and then we feel this wave of anxiousness and become imprisoned by our doubts, our worries, and the uncertainty of what dwells within tomorrow.

Maybe your childhood wasn't a field full of lilies or a peaceful time. Maybe you never felt that warmness of love, the tenderness of friendship, or gentleness and compassion from the beings who were present and appointed to protect you and keep you sheltered.

Those kids in the schoolyard weren't the cuddliest or the nicest. Your self-esteem hasn't been the same ever since you had that bad encounter with that one kid, or your teacher  made you feel as if you weren't smart enough, good enough, or capable enough to excel at being a better you.

You failed at that relationship. He said some harsh things, or she made you feel like you would never amount to anything. His words altered the perception of your beauty, and her actions altered your perception of your worth. The end left you bitter, the results aren't what you intended and now you're here, in this space, questioning love and its validity.

You are just like that baby elephant. Your circumstances have led you to believe that there is nothing to hope for, nothing to long for, and nothing left for you to believe in. You have been caged by your fears, bullied into a box of worthlessness and low self-esteem. Your relationships, your friendships, your human-to-human interactions have all been failed attempts at inclusion and vulnerability.

But maybe it's something else: the constant rejection, the relentless downward spirals that cause you to slip, trip, and fall each time you attempt to rise back up. Whatever it may be, that person, or thing, has had its ropes around you for far too long, and your evolution is depending on you to break the shackles that have kept you bound, stuck, fearful, and complacent with your crushing circumstances.

This isn't a story about knowing how to rise up out of your pain; it's about knowing how to walk into the fullness of freedom. Your life is no longer captive to the ones who used you, abused you, hurt you, or rejected you.

Freedom is a language that coexists with love, with compassion, with grace, and with steadfast humility. You have the weight and you have the strength to pull yourself away from anything that threatens your walk or evolution. Let no one, or thing, enslave you or keep you small for their benefit or gain. You are here. You are human. And you are alive.

Immerse yourself in knowing you have the power to alter your story, and your past does not have to dictate the outcome of your future. Whatever or whoever is holding you down—keep fighting, keep pulling, keep trying. Don't be like the baby elephant. Let nothing threaten your freedom; let today be the day that chains are broken, and your life begins to heal.

# Part II

# Dancing in the Dark

I had to learn how to love my darkness

    and revel in my weaknesses

just as much as I knew how

to love my victories.

I had to teach myself how to feel again

    in such an emotionally desolate world.

I touched my wounds and embraced the scars

that left behind evidence of

    my struggles within my life.

With that I learned true bravery;

I learned what true courage really looks like.

It was in the midst of

    my struggles that I learned

how to shine so eloquently in my

darkest moments.

# The Truth Is

You are allowed to be human; it is OK to be different, it is OK to not have it all together, and it is OK to fall flat on your face, stumble along the way, or fail over and over again. You are human, and you are wired to face difficulties. Our feelings fluctuate, our circumstances change, and our bodies react to particular situations as humanly as they should. We get scared, we cry a little or a lot, we get angry, sad, jealous, and annoyed—and there is nothing wrong with experiencing emotion.

The unbearable truth is—we all need help, and you don't have to be ashamed of that.

## Acceptance

I can't

experience

wholeness

if I am constantly

chipping away

pieces of myself

because I can't stand

to feel my own truths.

## Battlefield

Living in your mind

is not a safe place.

Get out of there.

## Free Yourself

As you press forward on your journey,

know that there is no amount of

    guilt, regret, shame, or remorse

powerful enough to resolve your past;

    only forgiveness can do that.

## You Are Not the Only One

I have experienced

a massive amount of

hurt and pain,

but so has he,

and so has she.

## Own Up to It

We live in a world where we are taught to suppress our emotions for the people who cannot handle our truths. We hide ourselves in fear of being "too much," "too serious," or "too emotionally unstable." But the more we walk away from our emotions, the further we get from our ability to be authentic.

We cannot give others what we don't give ourselves. Practicing vulnerability and authenticity equates to owning your feelings and tapping into your emotions.

We need to worry more about how we feel and less about what others think.

## How to Achieve Greatness

Find the courage to love yourself daily;

it'll be the greatest and most difficult task that you will ever pursue.

## False Identity

Life will always

    be a struggle

if you are constantly

    trying to live as a

person you were not created to be.

## Words to the Wise

Negativity will always obey its master. If you are emitting and absorbing negative frequencies, then they will travel to you and through you because you are calling out to them through your thoughts, words, and actions. Be mindful.

# Exploring Cities within Our Souls

We navigate through life with our stories and shared experiences. To live is to seek commonality, and to seek commonality means to be willing to share your story with your whole heart. Depression is a part of my story, and within that story are chapters about self-hate and poems on gliding blades across my wrists and turning blood into art and scars into beautifully aligned road maps. If you flip through the index of my soul, you will come across a young, broken, insecure, and frightened girl. You will find darkness and fear composed into sentences and hidden behind periods.

Truth and tragedy collide with one another as I unveil parts of myself that I never knew existed. The miraculous thing about storytelling is that we become fully present from our willingness to fully surrender. What once made us timid, we now recognize as our key to survival. The ultimate goal to happiness is the freedom to live as your most authentic self—to no longer be hidden behind shame, regret, your past, your mistakes, abuse, depression, neglect, and all other unfortunate circumstances. It takes time to piece your peace back together, but it also takes the courage to identify your truths and live in them without worrying about how others will perceive you.

A relationship with yourself requires open-heartedness, and a willingness to explore the virtues of love, grace, forgiveness, and compassion in order to truly grasp your worth. When you fully understand your worth, you understand all that is beautiful, and beauty serves as a portal to awaken the soul and strengthens your spine from all that has ever broken you down. We have to trust ourselves with the ability to live wholeheartedly without the approval of others and most certainly without the need to be loved by others. Love may not always be reciprocated from partners, friendships, or connections, but that does not water down your worth or your sense of belonging.

Our habits and our beliefs are at the core of how we choose to love ourselves and perceive ourselves. When our minds are made up about who we are, we live in that realm; believing that you are less than will allow you to put up with what you do not deserve. Telling yourself that things will never change serves as a barrier to growth because you are blocking change from accessing your soul. Be mindful of what you put out, because that is what you'll attract from the universe.

Connecting deeper with our spirit is the beginning of radical transformation. On a spiritual level, we are fighting with energies and forces that cannot be seen or heard, but they can be felt through our negative experiences. Love is rooted within the spirit. It is not just something that we feel; it is something that we do. It is the foundation of self-care.

Self-care is primary to your being, because without it you are left deficient and void of all virtues. You cannot live empty without grace, because that is how you touch yourself with compassion and give love to other beings. Grace is how our stories begin and should be how our stories end. When we choose to collaborate with our truths, we find love within our stories, and it is not followed by shame or regret.

Traveling beyond ourselves is the beginning of transformation. There is no way to predict what dwells outside of ourselves unless we have faith to trust the power of mystery and what lies within the unknown. Our hearts matter, and our stories matter; your story is valuable and worth telling, even if others choose not to listen. It is the road map that will lead you home, and it is your lesson, your compass, your poetry, your treasure, and the process of shedding yourself in order to become someone else.

## I Need You

Community says

I love you

when you are broken

fragile and delicate.

Community says

you don't have to suffer alone.

I have your back.

So let's do this thing called life together.

# Continue

Continue to spend time at coffee shops and getting lost in books.

Continue to travel distant places and explore the wonders of the world.

Continue to make those late-night phone calls that bring butterflies to your stomach.

Continue to visit museums and study the beauty of your art form and get to know your creator.

Continue to ride your bike, go for a swim, walk your dog, and be in tune with the everyday things that come with being human.

Continue to tell yourself that you are worthy.

Continue to tell yourself that your life deserves its best chance.

Continue to tell yourself that you are fearfully and wonderfully made.

Continue to show up for yourself with a full heart.

Continue so that you can continue, and then continue all over again.

## Dance like David

You are the drummer to the emotional rhythms that you feel.

When you allow yourself to dance within a force field of toxic energy and negativity, your movement becomes sluggish and the forces lingering around you weigh you down.

Increase your tempo and find the beat to the song in your heart that has a story to tell.

Be unapologetic as you move away from destruction into jubilated harmony, allowing the vibrations of your song to tingle down your spine.

Leap into a posture of praise, and keep dancing your way into victory…

Let no one steal your song.

Let no one steal your rhythm.

Let no one steal your joy.

Just keep dancing.

## Sailing

Life is a matter of how far are you willing to
go in order to give your life its best chance.

How much risk are you willing to take?

How deep are you willing to wander?

And what are you willing to go

oceans deep for?

To find love, peace, and wisdom

is about finding oneself

in unknown territory.


To extend yourself beyond what you know

is the beginning of transformation.

The moment that we align our footsteps

and walk among the path

that leads us away from the

familiar into the unfamiliar

is the moment that we shed ourselves

of who we once were in order to become

who we desire to be.

Allow your oceans to take you deeper,

trust your waves,

find your anchor,

and believe in the direction

you are sailing.

Go oceans deep

and embrace the unknown.

# Rich in Loss

Being lost is a gateway to surrender. When you acknowledge what you don't have, you can be fully immersed in what you do have. When you are fully grounded and present in the here and now, you gain a sense of wisdom that only being lost can provide you.

## A Place to Lie Down

I don't mean to crush you,

    but my bones are heavy.

I don't mean to smother you,

    but my limbs find their roots in you.

I darken everything I touch; I don't mean to.

The waves are rushing toward me; I need your saving

grace.

# A Meeting with My Creators

I want to go quietly,

I have found a place to sleep.

The river is calling me to go deeper,

the mountains are cheering for me to move,

the birds in the clouds dance for me,

and it feels so good to be celebrated,

to be welcomed,

to be wanted.

My heart will sleep well tonight.

## The Becoming

I struggled with the idea of being hopeful for so long.

My depression once suffocated me and anxiety crippled me.

My story consists of nights where I felt like my sky was broken and not one single star was shining. It consisted of many days where I felt as if the sun were hiding from me and exiled me to a world full of darkness.

When I took off my robe of shame and clothed myself in joy and unfiltered self-love, the world that once seemed so ugly became so beautiful. I no longer defined myself by my lack of shining stars, and I created my own solar system.

I became the light that I lacked. I became the love that I so desperately needed.

I became everything that I always desired to be, because I never gave up.

I learned that if I continue to believe that tomorrow will get better—

that is the greatest form of hope that I could ever have for myself.

# Absolution

There is an art to for(give)ness.

It's the ability to carry the wounds

of offense, debt, abuse,

transgression, and ridicule,

yet offer the inflictor

love, grace, mercy,

and compassion.

This is for your sake.

This is for your freedom.

## She and I Are Not Friends

She and I are not friends.

We tolerate each other.

We keep each other's secrets.

We remind each other of who we don't want to be.

We are more like acquaintances.

We actually dislike each other.

She and I could never be friends.

When she's around, my world feels small, my body is fragile, and I ache at the idea of living in the moment with her within my space.

But I hate walking alone. I'm bothered at the idea of living alone. I hate having conversations alone. I hate dwelling alone. I hate eating alone. I hate sleeping alone. I hate dancing alone. I hate being alone.

But we are not friends.

She and I are two cordial spirits lapsing through time.

She is a shadow. She is a disguise. She is a dream but also a nightmare.

She terrifies me. But her absence threatens me.

She awakens me. But she also disrupts my peace.

She discourages me. But she also gives me something to dream about.

She silences me. But she also gives me something to sing about.

She is a shadow. She is a disguise. She is a dream but also a nightmare.

I want to erase her. But I don't want to let her go.

When the world is dark, she helps me to find my light. And when the sun is illuminating the sky, she reminds me to honor and appreciate the darkness that has guided me to finding my true self.

She is a body of blackness.

Her face is blank, smudged, lifeless, and covered by

star like freckles.

I'm afraid of her. But I love her embrace.

Her hands are crystallized with an ember glow and she emits an energy so forceful that when her palms collide with your skin it sends vibrations of blazing warmth through your body.

She is not my friend.

She gives me so much yet depletes me of so much.

I hate her.

But I appreciate her.

She has blessed me with a gift.

She is masked as pain, but her heart doesn't know any better.

## Even When It Hurts like Hell

Be present...

Every morning when I awaken I speak these two words aloud like hymns being sung on a sweet Sunday morning. I reach for my journal and flood the pages with songs of hope and encouraging devotions as I prep myself for another day where I must learn to stand tall in the present moment. But regardless of what dwells in the mystery of today, my heart still beats for what lingers ahead within tomorrow.

Tomorrow has always been a significant day for me throughout life. See, tomorrow is the only motivation that I ever had to keep me alive through the nights when I believed my life wasn't worthy of its best chance. Struggling with depression while growing up made trying to get through the day an awful experience. Rising out of bed felt torturous, because if it were up to me, I would choose to waste away underneath my comforter. But even the sun has a way of passing judgment over us, for as its cheerfulness made its way through my window and looked upon me with its radiance, it would make me feel guilty about not making use of its light.

I hated activities, and I loved isolation. I enjoyed the present as long as I could be present with myself. People didn't understand me, and there came a point in my life where I felt as if I didn't understand people. They feared my depression just as much as I feared their happiness. I was afraid to experience the goodness of life, because in the back of my mind, it would only be a momentary high that could easily be snatched away from me without a reason.

The moment I began to struggle with self-injury, was a moment in my life when I realized that healing for me meant hoping for a better tomorrow. I considered myself a failure in life, and I ruled out any possibility of living boldly and bravely because depression told me that I wasn't good enough. All I could see, as I remained present, was a girl who was broken and searching for worthiness and love.

I wanted to believe that I could be better at this life and be greater than the lies that depression told me. As I struggled through the days, the only thing that gave me hope was the belief that today was shaping and preparing me for a greater tomorrow—a day where I would see the progress of my growth and recovery, a day where I could actively say I made the healthy decision to keep fighting, because for me tomorrow meant life or death. If I made it another day, that meant I made a choice to live—so fighting for tomorrow is the only thing that gave me hope and the courage to keep going even when the present hurt like hell.

I had a lot of fears about my trajectory of life. As a teen I wasn't sure if I would make it through high school, and when I accomplished that, I wasn't sure if I would make it through college, and when I accomplished that, I wasn't sure if I would manage life after the death of my father, but even through grief and loss, I found healing and managed through that. I wasn't sure if I had it in me to attend and complete graduate school, and when I graduated, I wasn't sure if I would have the perseverance and the confidence to trust the process of my journey and create the life I always wanted, but I went on and started a digital magazine because I wanted to fulfill the desires of my heart, and when I accomplished the launch of my business, I realized the power of living in the now while also fighting for tomorrow.

I'm twenty-six now, and I still have life, I still have breath. And that is because although depression stole my sight, it never stole my vision. I always longed for a livelier future; I just struggled with the process of getting there. At night I would always dream about what life would look like if I didn't have this illness—what would it feel like to love myself unconditionally, to not try to live up to a standard of perfection or play dress-up with personality traits in order to feel loved and included by the masses.

My healing process took years of therapy along with years of learning how to love every ounce of my body and the flesh that houses it. I had to fight for the girl I saw within the mirror, because deep within my heart, whenever I would wake to see another day, joy would fill my spirit because I could say I survived. I survived all that tormented me yesterday, and as I stand in the presence of today, I will be able to say the same thing tomorrow.

I've decided that practicing the art of being present means that I will cherish where I am in space and time, but I will also allow the experiences that unfold within the here and now to equip me for what lies ahead within tomorrow. My process has taught me that my struggles don't define me; they equip me for the journey. And the journey has shown me that my life is deserving of its best chance, and so is yours.

Be still and know that no matter how rough, taxing, or stressful today may be, I guarantee you will wake up to a better tomorrow. It may not feel that way, but admire your strength for allowing yourself to be vulnerable enough to expose yourself to the mystery of what dwells in another day, where you cannot control the outcome.

Keep fighting for tomorrow, believe in it, and

keep making plans for it. Keep reminding yourself that you have a reason to be alive, because tomorrow is your future, and that future you are fighting for can be made possible when you lay your head down to sleep in order to rise again. So be present. And give thanks to yesterday for equipping you for the journey and providing you with the hope and the healing that awaits for you today, and for tomorrow.

## Love Is

Love is gentle, it is pure, it's kind, it's authentic, and it's raw and uncut. Love sounds sweet, but once it is time to put love into practice and treat it as a duty to passionately embrace others with no judgment, no condemnation, no "I'm right" and "you're wrong" kind of attitude, is when you realize how great a responsibility love really is. Love understands that we are all imperfect people in need of grace and compassion; we need saving from ourselves because we are naturally vulnerable to failure and making mistakes. Love does not highlight shame, and it doesn't induce fear. It does not separate or segregate, it does not apply greater value to the color of one's skin, it does not degrade or diminish, and it is not to be toyed with out of convenience.

Love hard and with all that you've got. Don't treat people as if they are deserving of only half your heart, because there will be a time and a place where love will tell you good-bye when you are trying to say hello.

## No One Is Exempt

We all struggle in life.

No one is excluded from that.

It doesn't matter how wealthy you are.

It doesn't matter how religious you are.

It doesn't matter the color of your skin.

It doesn't matter what social class you fall under and

it doesn't matter how wise or intelligent you may be.

We are all susceptible to experiencing great pain and

misfortune,

because that is a part of the human experience.

## The Killing II

I killed myself a thousand times.

Rooted in so much hate.

Suppressing so much anger, cutting off my feelings, and avoiding my disappointments.

Never blooming. Never blossoming. Never staying fully alive.

I was afraid.

Afraid that if I grew away from you, your love would wither away.

But also afraid that if I stayed grounded, I would never truly be liberated.

Unwilling to experience my hurt and express my pain, I would rather have died than allow myself to flourish in the unknown.

The idea of what it would be like to lose your love would be too much of a tragedy.

So I killed myself a thousand times in order to preserve your love.

Dead for so long. Thirsty for freedom.

Homeless. Empty. Crippled and fragile.

I can't let my desire to love you be the death of me.

I may struggle to bloom on my own, and I may encounter endless storms, but I am ready to let go, to be free of you.

I am ready to see where my petals may fall and plant my seeds in the mystery of what losing your love may look like.

## Beginnings Are Always New

If your eyes are following these

words,

that means your lungs

are full of air,

and your mind is

lavished with

unconscious creativity.

You automatically get another

shot at doing

whatever the heck you want

with that beautiful life of yours.

And if you don't know

where to start,

feel free

to start here,

start now,

get going.

# The Invitation

This is an invitation to believe,

to be hopeful,

to have ridiculous faith.

This is an invitation for you to remain silent
and allow the universe to do the speaking for you.

Take off the mask.

Stop trying to be the person you think you should be,
and allow your soul to transform you into whom you
were created to be.

To the broken. To the lonely. To the lost and the
weary. To the hopeless ones and the faithless ones.

You are invited.

Let's take this journey into freedom together.

## It's Never Too Late

At times I question how deeply I have lived.

Did my faith move mountains?

Did I stand still in grace?

Did I love without condition?

Did I awaken every morning with

      gratitude for each breath?

Did I live unafraid of welcoming loneliness?

Did I learn how to attain happiness separate

    from circumstance?

So many questions.

I am not sure if I have the answers,

     but then I remember it's not too late.

I still have time to tend to the desires of my open
heart.

## Conversations with Nature

Don't allow your past

to smother or suffocate you,

said the sun.

There is always new air

to breathe and new life to receive.

Embracing your walk means letting go

of what was and being open to what will be.

My heart smiled.

## She and I Are Not Friends II

She and I are not friends.

I hate when I think about her, but she's always there, always here, always dwelling within my atmosphere.

I write about her.

But she knows what I am thinking.

Her presence is potent when I am dreaming.

She breathes on me, and I shiver from her coldness.

She's no committed partner. I am not her only victim.

She and I are not friends, but she also is not my enemy.

I've learned how to go from broken to whole because of her.

I've learned how to go from bitter to forgiving because of her.

I've learned how to go from fragile to healed because of her.

I've learned how to live without regret because of her.

I've learned how to be gentle with myself because of her.

She has evolved my weaknesses into my strengths.

She and I are not friends.

We tolerate each other.

We keep each other's secrets.

She reminds me of who I don't want to be.

## The Art of Letting Go

It's not hard to decipher what is wrong for you;

what's hard is letting go.

## Come Home

Often, we go searching for ourselves

In people.

In places.

In things.


Forgetting that the true self is

found within the bones.

In the heart.

In the mind.

In the soul.

In the body.

## The Death of Me

My lungs are on fire,

I told God to rebuke my tongue and let me choke on my words anytime I forget to speak about myself in a manner of grace and kindness.

When I forget about his mercy, I ask God to shatter my heart into pieces so that I can feel what he feels and ache how he aches.

I said, let me feel your pain…

Let me feel your pain when I speak recklessly of your name, and belittle my being when I forget from where I came.

He laughs at me.

He says go back to the river.

Go drown in my grace.

## Valley of Dry Bones

My life is living proof that second chances

do come from dead things.

## The Wild

Every day we are passing through the
rummages of something that did not work out
well.

Every day we are unraveling, disconnecting.
Disentangling, separating, and unweaving
from the very thing that we once believed
made us whole.

As we travel toward healing, we are prone to
experience setbacks because that is just the
way the universe works.

All the small things gather around waiting to
attack your energy field.

All the shattered pieces that were never swept
up look for a place to call home.

All the madness that was silenced and
discarded searches for a healthy mind to

befriend and unpack its burdens.

And all that was forgotten forces its way in,
demanding to be remembered.

Even the rainfall looks for a place to flood.

But despite the rising of the tide and the
outpouring of nature's sorrows—you are to
remain rooted like the flower.

You must not bend nor break; you simply
transform and face the overwhelming forces
and streams that you cannot control.

You recognize your cultivated beauty and
your intricate art form—and you let no one
pluck or plunder at your petals.

You stay grounded in your seasons; growth is
essential to your livelihood, and disrupting the
process is disrespectful to the soul.

On the other side of pain and discomfort is

the arrival of joy and healing.

And as you continue to search through all that
is unraveling you,

trust that those same rivers that you thought
were here to drown you

can actually make you whole.

MINAA B.

# About the Author

Minaa B. who was born Jessmina Archbold, is an LMSW, mental health consultant and advocate, and the CEO/founder of the digital magazine Respect Your Struggle. She has been published in mediums such as Too Write Love on Her Arms and ThinkProgress, and she is a freelance writer for the Huffington Post and Conscious magazine. Minaa was born and raised in Queens, New York, graduated from Briarcliffe College with Her bachelor's degree in business administration, and later received her master of social work degree from New York University.

Visit: www.minaab.com

Respect Your Struggle: www.respectyourstruggle.com

E-mail: fromminaab@gmail.com

Follow: @Minaa_B on Instagram |

@MinaaBe on Twitter

Made in the USA
San Bernardino,
CA